CHICAGO

A PICTURE MEMORY

Text
Bill Harris

Captions
Louise Houghton

Design
Teddy Hartshorn

Photography
Colour Library Books Ltd
FPG International
George Freston
International Stock Photo

Picture Research
Annette Lerner

Commissioning Editor
Andrew Preston

Editorial
Jane Adams
Gill Waugh

Production
Ruth Arthur
David Proffit
Sally Connolly

Director of Production
Gerald Hughes

Director of Publishing
David Gibbon

CLB 2510

This 1990 edition is published by Crescent Books,
distributed by Outlet Book Company, Inc., a Random House Company,
40 Engelhard Avenue, Avenel, New Jersey 07001.

Random House
New York • Toronto • London • Sydney • Auckland

Printed and bound in Singapore

ISBN 0-517-01752-0

10 9 8 7 6 5 4

CHICAGO

A PICTURE MEMORY

CRESCENT BOOKS
New York / Avenel, New Jersey

First page: the Buckingham Memorial Fountain, built by Kate Buckingham in memory of her brother Clarence in 1927. Previous pages: the incomparable Chicago waterfront and (facing page) Sears Tower seen from Kinzie Street Bridge.

It's time to get a few things straight about Chicago. It is not unusually windy. It is neither a second city nor a second-rate city. It is not overrun with gangsters. Moreover, it is not the capital of the kind of dullness so many people associate with middle America. Rather, it is at the center of sophisticated American thought, and has been so for generations.

Even people who can't find Chicago on a map are able to identify it as "the windy city." Yet how about about Kansas City? The average windspeed in Chicago may be 10.2 mph, but it's 10.7 mph in Kansas City. If you follow the shore of Lake Michigan up to Milwaukee, the wind's average 11.6 mph will knock your hat into the creek and, if you take a steamer from Chicago to Buffalo, the wind's 12 mph will bowl you over. Even in terms of record gusts, Chicago is far down the list. The highest wind speed recorded in St. Louis was 60 mph, but that was the moment the gauge blew away. Chicago's record is 58 mph. Even New York, whose average wind speeds are less than a mile an hour slower than Chicago's, has recorded a high of 70 mph.

It was a New Yorker who pinned the name on the city at the end of Lake Michigan. But he wasn't thinking of Chicago's climate. As the year 1892 came into sight, promoters smelled an opportunity to celebrate the 400th anniversary of the discovery of America, and the competition for the honor was between New York and Chicago. It was a bitter fight, which Chicago won because its political leaders were able to talk for longer and more often in places where words mattered most. The debate prompted Charles Dana to write in *The New York Sun* that no one should listen to "the nonsensical claims of the windy city." Although Dana and other New Yorkers thought Chicagoans were full of hot air, no one seemed to care west of the Hudson River.

Having lost that battle, New York tried again fifty years later when A.J. Leibling told readers of *The New Yorker Magazine* that Chicago was America's "second city." This label became a kind of badge of honor in Chicagoland, where everyone knows the city is second to none.

Out in Los Angeles, which replaced Chicago as America's second-largest city in the 1980s, the image-makers have been working for generations to make everybody think that Chicago is overrun by gangsters. Even though it's probably safer to walk alone on Michigan Avenue than on Hollywood Boulevard, visitors to Chicago still can't resist the urge to look over their shoulders to see if George Raft and Claire Trevor are among their fellow strollers.

Actually, the Prohibition-era mobsters who made Elliot Ness famous and gave Hollywood so much inspiration were parvenus. Around the turn of the century, a London newspaper was already telling its readers that "other places hide their blackness out of sight. Chicago treasures it in the heart of the business district and gives it a veneer."

The business district they were writing about was the First Ward, a section of town known in those days as the Levee because most of the businesses there were owned by transplanted Southern gamblers. A person could get anything at all on the Levee, including a bump on the head and an empty wallet. They say there were more than 200 brothels in the neighborhood, and not one was hidden behind discreet red lights. The in spot was run by Ike Bloom, who made more money from his girls than from his booze, and made it a point to get his name in the papers as often as possible to make sure his joint kept its number one status.

The First Ward was represented at City Hall by a pair of aldermen named Hinky Dink Kenna and Bathhouse John Coughlin. Together, and for a price, they kept the climate cool, so to speak. Their partnership lasted nearly fifty years, during which time they each built up a tidy fortune by demanding payoffs. It was said that Bathhouse was the best-dressed man in America, and it was best said by the Bath himself, when someone compared him to the then Prince of Wales. "When it comes to mapping out style for well-dressed Americans," he responded, "the Prince is simply a faded two-spot in the deck of fashion."

Hinky Dink was no sartorial slouch himself but, as a true believer in thrift, he saved for the future. He did take a trip to Europe once but, when he got back, the best thing he could say about Rome was that "most everybody there has been dead for two thousand years."

By contrast, Hink had a lot of Italian constituents in the First Ward, who were very much alive. Among these was Big Jim Colosimo, a restaurant owner who had lured the likes of Enrico Caruso to the Levee to sample the spaghetti. Big Jim also sold protection to bordello owners, a sideline that was much more profitable than pasta. Though Hinky Dink Kenna much preferred rubbing elbows with the Irish residents of the Ward, he was nothing if not a practical man, and so he made an alliance with Colosimo. Big Jim got protection from City

Hall, and Hink got blocks of votes guaranteed, as well as the loyal services of enforcers who could keep the ward in line. It was a perfect arrangement: Big Jim had a free reign without having to worry about buying cops one at a time, while Hink expanded his power, but kept his respectability. What more could a politician ask for?

More power is probably the correct answer to that question. However, as very young men, both Hink and the Bath had decided that the secret of success in their chosen field, and the best way to stay out of jail, was to stay small. "We leave Washington graft to congressmen," one of them once said. "There's less risk in the small stuff and in the long run, it pays a damn sight more."

They may have found an advantage in thinking small, but neither Hink nor the Bath were small-timers. Their proudest achievement was the annual First Ward Ball, a social event of staggering proportions that also served as a charity affair, the beneficiaries being Kenna, Coughlin and the local Democratic Party. The ball was Bathhouse John's idea in the first place, and he threw himself into organizing it with single-minded enthusiasm. He even wrote the music for the bands to play, including such immortal hits as *Why Did They Build The Lake So Near The Shore?*, and *They're Tearing Up Clark Street Again*.

All the business people in the ward, from saloonkeepers to bordello owners, had the arm put on them to buy blocks of tickets. Brewers and distillers were expected to make contributions to the bar. Waiters even paid Bathhouse John for the privilege of working at the frolic. The most spectacular of all the First Ward Balls was the one held in 1908. Bathhouse John showed up in a tuxedo with purple lapels, worn with a bright red sash. The hatcheck girl, who gave him a tip for choosing her, got to hang up his yellow overcoat and red scarf and took special care not to lose his pink kid gloves. The working girls from the Levee didn't show up until after their work was over, of course. It was worth the wait though, because they came in costume. The most popular costume that year was the Egyptian look, a holdover from the recent Centennial Exposition, when a dancer called Little Egypt had helped spread Chicago's fame. Whatever the costume, short skirts were the common denominator. *The Tribune* reported that this was because "It was bad form to wear anything that might collect germs from the floor."

Hinky Dink's assessment of the party was "It's a lollapalooza! ... Chicago ain't no sissy town!" He was absolutely right; but Chicago hadn't seen anything yet.

By the end of 1908, Chicagoans had become a little weary of the shenannigans in the First Ward and they began clamoring for reform. A religious revival swept through town at about the same time and a year or two later, the Levee was dark and comparatively dull. Most of the entrepreneurs either retired or went into less flamboyant businesses. Some of them, however, were too old to learn new trades.

Among these was Big Jim Colosimo, who decided to go underground until the heat was off. That made him a target for potential rivals, so he went to New York and hired a bodyguard, an eager young fellow named Johnny Torrio. Johnny was as smart as he was tough, and it wasn't long before he was bigger than his boss. In a stroke of marketing genius, he reasoned that the automobile would take business away from the center city, and conned Big Jim into giving him exclusive rights to operate in the suburbs. By 1912, towns like Cicero, Hammond and Calumet City were Torrio country, and boasted a string of roadhouses where a steelworker could get just about anything on his way home. All this kept Johnny so busy that it slipped his mind he was also Colosimo's bodyguard. And that was the end of Big Jim.

Torrio filled the vacuum created by Colosimo's untimely death himself, of course, so now he needed a bodyguard of his own. He found his man in the person of a fellow New Yorker calling himself Al Brown. Early in his career, a Chicago newspaper identified him as Alfred Caponi. It wasn't long before they got it right – the man was Alphonse Capone. They didn't come any tougher. Any kid who had grown up on New York's Lower East Side with a name like Alphonse had to be tough.

When Al arrived in Chicago, he brought an old fishbowl, a couple of chairs, a piano and other assorted junk and opened a secondhand furniture store on Wabash Avenue. There is no record of whether he ever sold any of the stuff. Indeed, there is no record of Al ever earning any money, but it's obvious he made plenty of it. Some years after his arrival, when the Federal Government charged him with income tax evasion, they based their claim on an income of $1,050,000 between 1924 and 1929. But they were just guessing, and the guess was clearly conservative, because, at one point during the trial, the judge was offered $1,500,000 to let Al go free.

The Government only had itself to blame for giving Capone an opportunity to make that kind of money. In 1920, the year that Al arrived in Chicago, the selling and drinking of alcoholic beverages became illegal. Torrio grabbed the opportunity, buying up breweries and raising the price of beer to fifty dollars a barrel. Once he owned all the breweries, the price went even higher.

Although they had cornered the market in beer, Johnny and Al had plenty of competition in other areas of their business. In the early days, most of this competition came from Dion O'Banion, a North State Street florist who controlled the wealthiest parts of the city – politicians, speakeasies, cops, gambling dens, the works. One day O'Banion was found dead with five bullets in his chest and a sixth in his head. Capone and Torrio showed up at the funeral, one of the biggest America had ever seen but, as soon as the ceremonies were over, Torrio went on the run. O'Banion's henchmen were hot on his trail, following him all the way to Havana and then back to Chicago, where they shot him dead on his own front porch. After that it was up to Al to carry the load all by himself.

The battle for control lasted four years. During that time a lot of people died violently in Chicago, and a lot of other people blamed Al Capone. As he himself put it, "I've been accused of every death except the casualty list of the World War."

His archenemies were the six Genna brothers, who had a Government permit to distill industrial alcohol. To improve production, they imported laborers from their native Sicily, who were paid fifteen dollars a day in return for a promise to operate stills in their apartments. More than 100 families took the Gennas up on the offer, and the brothers opened a warehouse on State Street to keep the public supplied. Theirs was the biggest store on the street, and the Genna brothers became very rich indeed. Capone eliminated three of the brothers in the space of a few weeks, and the other three got the message that it was time to go home to Sicily. Now all Al had to worry about was Bugs Moran and the remnants of the O'Banion gang.

The battle ended dramatically on February 14, 1929, when five men, three of them dressed in police uniforms, walked into a Clark Street garage and mowed down seven of Moran's men. When the real police arrived on the scene after the perpetrators had vanished, one of the victims, not quite dead yet, told them, "No one done it. No one shot me." Nevertheless, the whole world thought that Al Capone had done it. The St. Valentine's Day massacre, as it became known, brought him international fame and undisputed control of Chicago.

No one was ever able to pin anything on Al Capone but, a few years later, the Fed accused him of avoiding income taxes, sentenced him to eleven years in prison and collected a fine of $75,000. Al was shocked at what he called a "blow below the belt." He told a reporter, "They are prejudiced against me. I never had a chance."

A bum rap? Probably not. The real injustice was probably that suffered by Chicago itself. Al Capone wasn't even born in the city whose less notorious natives would make any city proud.

In today's world of transistorized communications, it's easy to forget that the vacuum tube made radio possible, and that it was invented in Chicago by a tinkerer named Lee DeForest. When people began staying home with their radios, they spent their happiest hours listening to broadcasts from Chicago by Freeman Gosden and Charles Correll, better known as Amos N' Andy. Once television came along, Chicago gave it the style that people still call its golden age through performers like Dave Garroway and Burr Tillstrom, who gave us Kukla, Fran and Ollie.

Chicago gave the world its skyscrapers, too. The first of them was William Jenny's Home Insurance Company Building; the best of them were built by the firms of Burnham and Root and by Louis Sullivan, still regarded as one of the best architects America has ever produced. Best, that is, if you discount Frank Lloyd Wright, one of Sullivan's pupils.

Chicago produced journalistic legends like Ring Lardner, Ben Hecht and Carl Sandburg. H.L. Mencken, who knew a good writer when he saw one, said, "Find a writer who is indubitably an American in every pulsebeat, snort and adenoid, an American who has something new and peculiarly American to say and who says it in an unmistakably American way and nine times out of ten you'll find that he has some sort of connection with that gargantuan and inordinate abattoir by Lake Michigan ... that he was bred there, or got his start there, or passed through there in the days when he was young and tender. In Chicago, a spirit broods upon the face of the waters."

Even if your taste runs more to the funny papers, you still owe a big debt to Chicago. Gasoline Alley, to which three generations of Americans turned every week to watch a kid named Skeezix grow up, was in Chicago. Dick Tracy comes from Chicago, too. It was in Chicago that Buck Rogers first saw the future. The Toonerville Trolley rattled and rolled off a Chicago drawing board, and it was in a Chicago office that Winnie Winkle did her thing as "the breadwinner," years before working women became fashionable. The list of comic strip characters created in Chicago includes Little Orphan Annie and Moon Mullins, Steve Canyon and Terry and The Pirates.

Chicago has been known for years as "the city that works." It's big, and has all the problems other big cities have, but it also has a remarkable small-town quality, and that's why it works so well. It's a solid, hard-working place that is probably more American than any other spot in America. At night, the downtown streets are safer than in most other cities, and are possibly more exciting than in any of them. And yes, the natives are friendly. They're proud, too, because there's plenty to be proud of in Chicago. It contains the world's biggest airport and the world's tallest building. It boasts the finest hotels and restaurants. It houses the stockyards and the Merchandise Mart and a stock exchange that almost rivals New York's. It's a center for advertising and entertainment, not to mention printing and manufacturing. It produces almost as much steel as Pittsburgh; it's the world's biggest railroad center, and the largest port on the Great Lakes.

If other American cities look down their noses at Chicago, they should remember that, without it, their buildings probably wouldn't be more than five stories high, they wouldn't be able to get advice from "Dear Abby," they wouldn't have a Sears catalogue to make their wishes come true, and where in the world would they get their "New York Cut" steaks?

Yet Chicago is much more than the sum of all these parts. The city has a frontier spirit that shows up in its friendly, eager people. It is meant to impress you, and it usually succeeds. Even Rudyard Kipling, who didn't mind saying that he wasn't at all impressed by Chicago, couldn't help admitting that: "I have struck a city ... a real city ... and they call it Chicago. The other places do not count."

Facing page: downtown Chicago, the site of the first and the biggest skyscraper in the world.

Despite the fact that the entire extent of the city's public sector, except the Chicago Water Tower (below), was destroyed in the Great Fire of 1871, Chicago has long been famous for its architecture. The destruction held an irresistible attraction for the top designers of the time, who flocked in and began the creation of the city as it is today. Louis Sullivan found it "magnificent and wild: a crude extravaganza, an intoxicating rawness, a sense of things to be done" when he arrived to ply his trade shortly after the fire. Modern and historic structures stand shoulder to shoulder, at once a standard of things past and a promise of the stability of the brave new world. "Big Stan", the eighty-story Standard Oil Building (left), was completed in 1974 and is constructed of Italian marble, whilst 333 Wacker Drive (below left) shows a reflective, rounded face to the Illinois sky. Walking south down Michigan Avenue, or the "Magnificent Mile", from the Water Tower one comes across the Wrigley Building and the Tribune Tower, two of the city's most impressive structures (bottom left). Marina City (facing page) is another example of innovative design, some of its balconied apartments enjoying a bird's eye view of the George Washington, Robert Morris, Haym Salomon Memorial in Heald Square. Overleaf: the city by the lake.

Michigan Avenue (these pages and overleaf) is known and revered throughout the world as an example of harmonious inner-city development. The Wrigley Building (facing page, above and right) is a particularly fine Spanish Renaissance structure based upon the Geralda Tower of Madrid's Escorial, whilst the dramatically terminated tower of the Associates Building (below) will please the eye of the lover of more modern architecture. Above: the Hancock Center stands like a sentinel.

The State of Illinois Center (these pages) was completed in 1985 and is of truly innovative design. Vast and full of light, the extravagance of the public building was criticized by some, but not by the Governor of Illinois, who proclaimed it a "twenty-first-century work."

19

Mexican Independence Day is celebrated in style in Chicago; traditional dress, music, flags and parades enliven the streets.

Chicagoans love large scale sculpture. Contemporary and conservative works of art share prominent positions in the city's plazas and parks and boast well-known signatures. Below: a sculpture by Pablo Picasso, (above right) a work by Marc Chagall, (above) Claes Oldenburg's Batcolumn, (facing page bottom) Alexander Calder's Flamingo, and (facing page top) Lorado Taft and Leonard Crunelle's memorial in Heald Square. Overleaf: the Wrigley Building and Gothic-style Tribune Tower on Michigan Avenue.

Chinks of light form a mosaic of florescent colors (these pages and overleaf) as night falls in Chicago. Red tail-lights stripe the streets and the windows of earnest office workers shine on past the light of day.

The joy of living in Chicago owes a lot to the city's waterside location. The real estate on Lake Shore Drive (this page) is much coveted and sells at a high premium. Sunbathing and jogging come free. Achsah Bond Drive (facing page bottom) leads to the John G. Shedd Aquarium, the largest indoor aquarium in the world. Facing page top: Lincoln Park Zoo, set in thirty-five acres and highly esteemed for its captive, and captivating, gorillas.

The pulse of Chicago beats to the rhythm of the elevated railroad system downtown at the "Loop" (these pages). This bustling business and shopping district is less than a square mile in area, yet uniquely and evocatively Chicagoan. The linear grids of iron and concrete filter the Illinois sky and splash the sidewalks with light. Overleaf: the north shore of the Chicago River. The ornate Tribune Tower is an example of Gothic Revival style, its top a replica of the south tower of Rouen Cathedral.

The Mercantile Exchange (these pages and overleaf) at 444 West Jackson Boulevard is the world's largest market for perishable commodities, where traders deal in a variety of goods including eggs, cattle and pork bellies! The hi-tech resources are utilized to full advantage in the mayhem characteristic of a day at the exchange. Visitors may watch the action from a gallery on weekdays.

Adler Planetarium (below), on a promontory in Lake Michigan that affords possibly the best view of the city (bottom left), answers all the questions you ever wanted to ask about the universe and poses many more. Other fascinating places to visit include the Field Museum of Natural History (above) and Chinatown (left). The Hancock Center (facing page) on North Michigan Avenue is the sixth tallest building in the world, its bulk nudging 1,130 feet in height. Above left: the Chicago Cubs seek a keen following.

With so much water around their city, Chicagoans are indulged in their love for boating. Lake Michigan (these pages) is so big that to all intents and purposes it is a sea. Yachting is a popular sport and the Burnham Park (right and below), Monroe (facing page bottom) and Chicago (overleaf) harbors provide moorings for many a fine craft and present a pleasing spectacle to the onlooker. A picturesque sternwheeler (bottom right) may be found by Navy Pier, Grand Avenue, keeping the balance between the old and the new on the water just as it is maintained on shore.

Nothing if not lively, Chicago lights up at night both literally and metaphorically: neon signs (above) glow boldly, illuminated fountains (below) shoot skywards like champagne, and, on Michigan Avenue (facing page and oveleaf), trees are dusted with tiny bulbs. Chicago's small bars (above left) and shops (below left) have a character and charm all of their own. Left: bright paintwork on nearby old buildings brightens up the walk under the "El" tracks.

Dramatic early evening skies (these pages and overleaf) range in tone from palest pastel to forbidding darkness as the street lights come on and the stars come out over Chicago. Aerial views of the city clearly reveal the flatness of the surrounding area, and a view from Lake Michigan (right) plots a graph-like image of the city's skyscrapers as they vie for supremacy.

In a city with a river running through it bridges are inevitably a feature, and this is certainly true of Chicago, with its ever-present flow of traffic. The traffic isn't all on the roads though, and cars may have to give way to a boat or two as the barriers come down on *Michigan Avenue (facing page), Kinzie Street (left), Clark Street (below)* or *Wabash Avenue (overleaf)* bridges. Chicago has long been known for its newspapers, at one time producing a total of seventeen! Today only the Chicago Tribune *and the* Chicago Sun-Times remain, their offices enjoying central, riverside locations *(facing page and overleaf).* Many people have had their start, one way or another, in the newspaper business in Chicago; Al Capone himself liked to brag about his first break as hired muscle in the circulation wars.

The Metropole Hotel (facing page), where Al Capone had his headquarters during his reign of terror in the 1920s, records this mobster's many-faceted life of crime, including details of the St. Valentine's Day massacre on Clark Street (below). Finally imprisoned for tax evasion, Capone was estimated to have made $105 million from gambling and prostitution rackets in the year 1927. These days, with "Scarface" and many of his friends gone, Chicago's police force (this page) goes about its business with a little less trepidation.

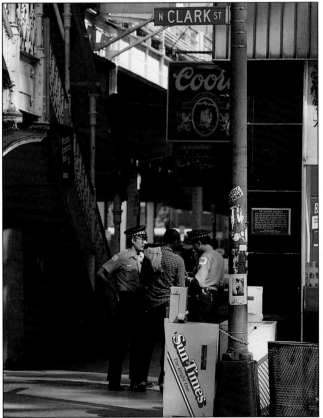

The buildings that make the city great do so by more than height alone. Below: the evening sun glows gold on the curve of 333 Wacker Drive as it echoes a bend in the Chicago River. Sears Tower (left and facing page) doesn't know what it means to look up – at 1,454 feet it is the world's tallest building. Overleaf: the city in all its illuminated glory. Following page: the Hancock Center, the world's largest combined office and apartment building.